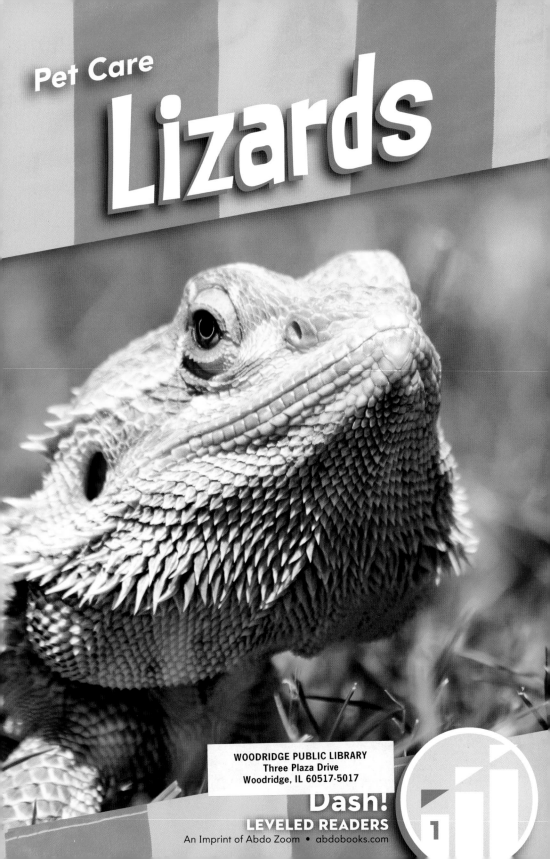

# Pet Care
# Lizards

## Dash!
### LEVELED READERS
An Imprint of Abdo Zoom • abdobooks.com

1

# Dash!
## LEVELED READERS

### Level 1 – Beginning
Short and simple sentences with familiar words or patterns for children who are beginning to understand how letters and sounds go together.

### Level 2 – Emerging
Longer words and sentences with more complex language patterns for readers who are practicing common words and letter sounds.

### Level 3 – Transitional
More developed language and vocabulary for readers who are becoming more independent.

## abdobooks.com

Published by Abdo Zoom, a division of ABDO, PO Box 398166, Minneapolis, Minnesota 55439.
Copyright © 2019 by Abdo Consulting Group, Inc. International copyrights reserved in all countries.
No part of this book may be reproduced in any form without written permission from the publisher.
Dash!™ is a trademark and logo of Abdo Zoom.

Printed in the United States of America, North Mankato, Minnesota.
092018
012019

Photo Credits: iStock, Shutterstock
Production Contributors: Kenny Abdo, Jennie Forsberg, Grace Hansen, John Hansen
Design Contributors: Dorothy Toth, Neil Klinepier

Library of Congress Control Number: 2018945715

## Publisher's Cataloging in Publication Data

Names: Murray, Julie, author.
Title: Lizards / by Julie Murray.
Description: Minneapolis, Minnesota : Abdo Zoom, 2019 | Series: Pet care |
    Includes online resources and index.
Identifiers: ISBN 9781532125249 (lib. bdg.) | ISBN 9781641856690 (pbk) |
    ISBN 9781532126260 (ebook) | ISBN 9781532126772 (Read-to-me ebook)
Subjects: LCSH: Lizards--Juvenile literature. | Lizards as pets--Juvenile
    literature. | Pets--Juvenile literature. | Lizards--Behavior--Juvenile literature.
Classification: DDC 639.395--dc23

# Table of Contents

# Lizards

Lizards can make great pets.
They come in many colors.
Chameleons can change
their colors.

Lizards can be big or small. Green iguanas can grow to be 3-6 feet (.9-1.8 m) long!

Lizards do not like to be petted. Some lizards are OK being handled, while others are not.

Handle a lizard very gently. Never pick it up by its tail. Its tail can break off! But it will grow back.

Lizards can carry certain **bacteria**. Be sure to wash your hands after touching a lizard.

Lizards need a **terrarium**. It is a special cage. It needs to be kept clean.

Lizards are **cold-blooded**. They need a special light to keep them warm.

Some lizards need branches to climb. Some need dry sand. Others need water to lie in. Green anoles need a place to hide.

Some lizards eat fruits or greens. Others like to eat worms and insects. Bearded dragons eat crickets!

# Things Lizards Need

- Fresh food and water

- A clean **terrarium**

- A special light to keep warm

- Branches, sand, and rocks for climbing and hiding

# Glossary

**bacteria** – a microscopic organism that can cause disease.

**cold-blooded** – having blood whose temperature changes with the temperature of the air or water. Animals such as snakes, fish, and lizards are cold-blooded.

**terrarium** – a closed container for keeping small animals, usually made of clear glass.

# Index

accessories 17, 18

bearded dragon 20

chameleon 4

cleaning 12, 15

color 4

food 20

green anole 18

green iguana 7

handling 8, 11

personality 8

size 7

tail 11

terrarium 15, 17, 18

# Online Resources

**Booklinks**
**NONFICTION NETWORK**
FREE! ONLINE NONFICTION RESOURCES

To learn more about lizard care, please visit **abdobooklinks.com**. These links are routinely monitored and updated to provide the most current information available.